JOHN ADAMS
OPERA CHORUSES

VOLUME 2

CHORUSES FROM NIXON IN CHINA, DOCTOR ATOMIC, A FLOWERING TREE

EDITED BY GRAN

HENDON MUSIC

www.boosey.com

The first time I met John Adams I was playing piano rehearsals for *Nixon in China*. The year was 1990 and I remember vividly both the unbridled joy of discovering his work for the first time and the utter terror that my counting would go awry, and I'd fall into one of those infamous "John Adams holes" where one careens full-bore into a beat of (intended) silence. John was extraordinarily kind to me in those rehearsals and he clearly had a sense of how crazy it is to corral an entire orchestra's worth of activity into 10 fingers! That began a long and treasured friendship, and I have an enduring love, based on those early experiences, of hearing John's operas and oratorios played on the piano.

Over the past 30 years I've played, conducted, and in several cases, premiered John's works with continued joy and (maybe slightly) less terror. As a pianist and conductor with a deep love of choirs I've often wished that there was more music of John's available to choral ensembles. John seems to pour heart and soul into the choruses of his large-scale works and so it has been frustrating that only those choral ensembles lucky enough to be associated with a symphony orchestra or opera company have heretofore had access to this great repertoire. I'm therefore delighted that these newly transcribed versions of some of John's greatest choruses will open up his music to many more choral ensembles and pianists.

I'm hugely grateful to Zizi Mueller for envisioning and championing this undertaking, and to Maggie Heskin for shepherding it through to completion. We recently "test drove" several of these transcriptions in concert with the Los Angeles Master Chorale and I'm deeply indebted for both the brilliant playing and the honest feedback from our four rock star pianists—Gloria Cheng, Lisa Edwards, Bryan Pezzone and Vicki Ray. Most of all I am in awe of Chitose Okashiro for wrestling the unbridled inventiveness of John's orchestral writing into 88 keys, two hands and 10 digits! These transcriptions are imaginative, colorful, and of course fantastically virtuosic. I hope that through them and through this edition John Adams' great choral music will resonate with adventurous choral ensembles far and wide!

—Grant Gershon

CONTENTS

SOLDIERS OF HEAVEN
from NIXON IN CHINA

Libretto by
ALICE GOODMAN

Piano reduction by
CHITOSE OKASHIRO

Music by
JOHN ADAMS

979-0-051-48573-4

Printed 2020

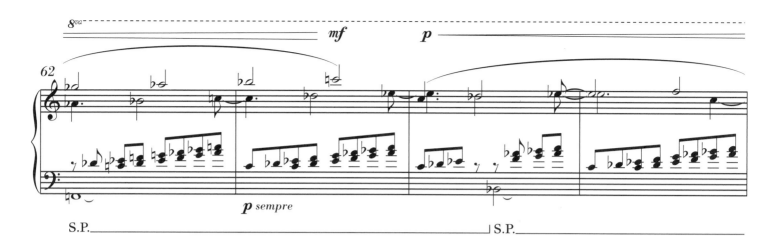

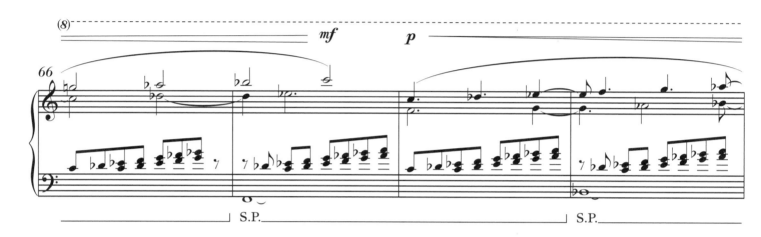

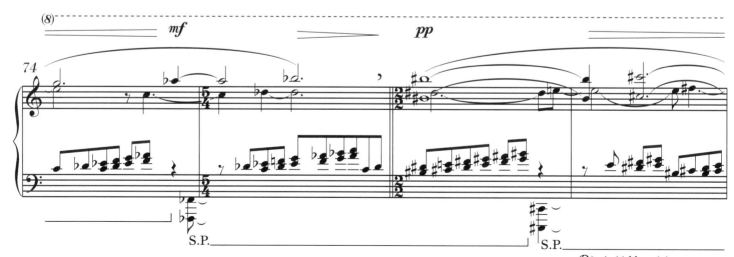

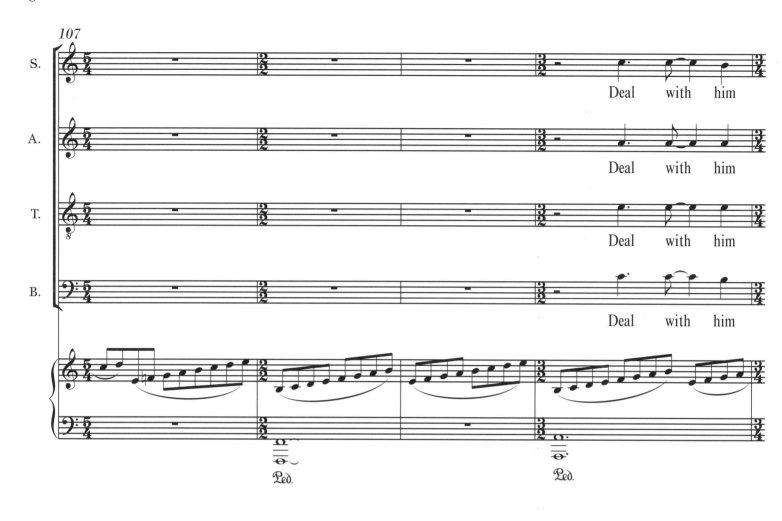

peas-ant's plow.

FLESH REBELS
from NIXON IN CHINA

Libretto by
ALICE GOODMAN

Music by
JOHN ADAMS

Piano reduction by
CHITOSE OKASHIRO

Female
Chorus

Female
Chorus

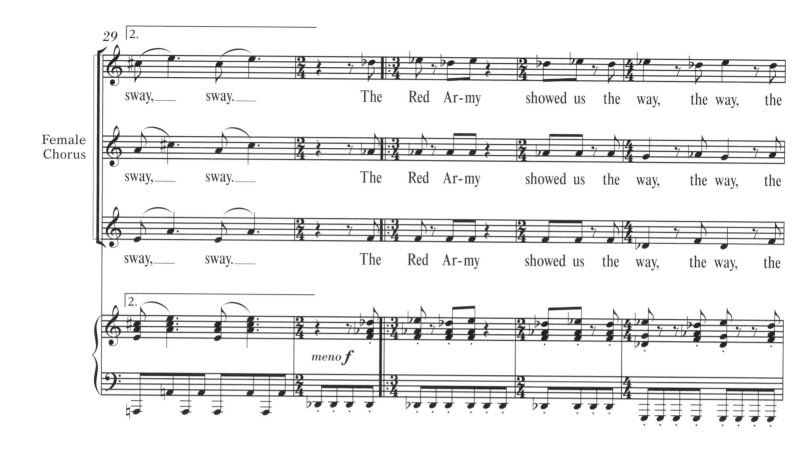

CHEERS
from NIXON IN CHINA

Libretto by
ALICE GOODMAN

Piano reduction by
CHITOSE OKASHIRO

Music by
JOHN ADAMS

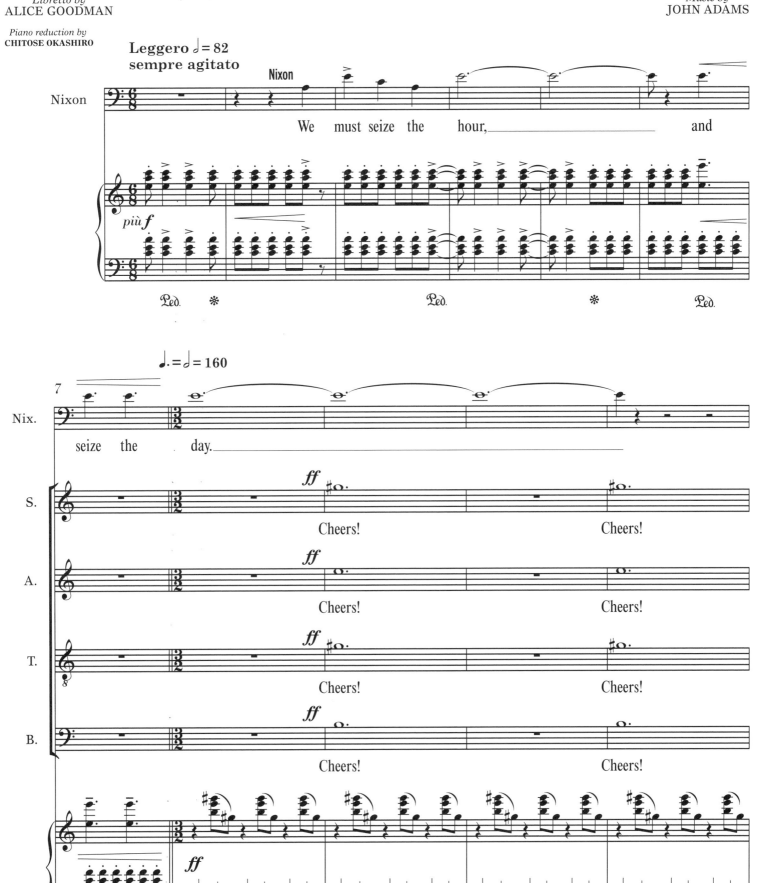

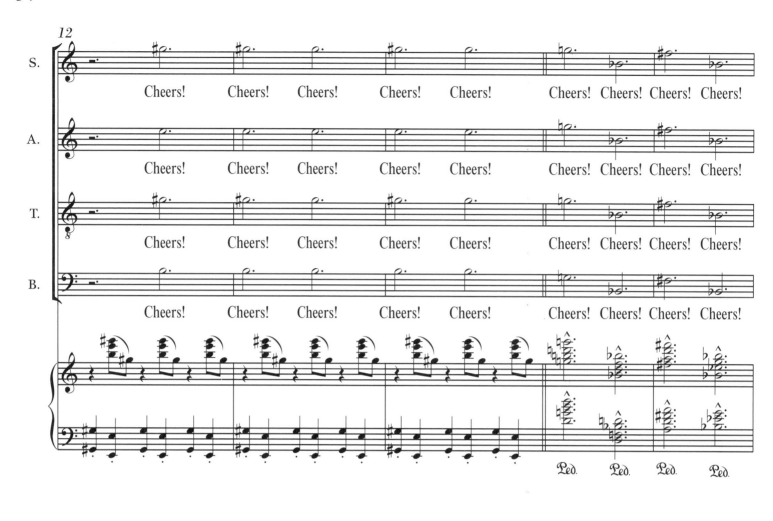

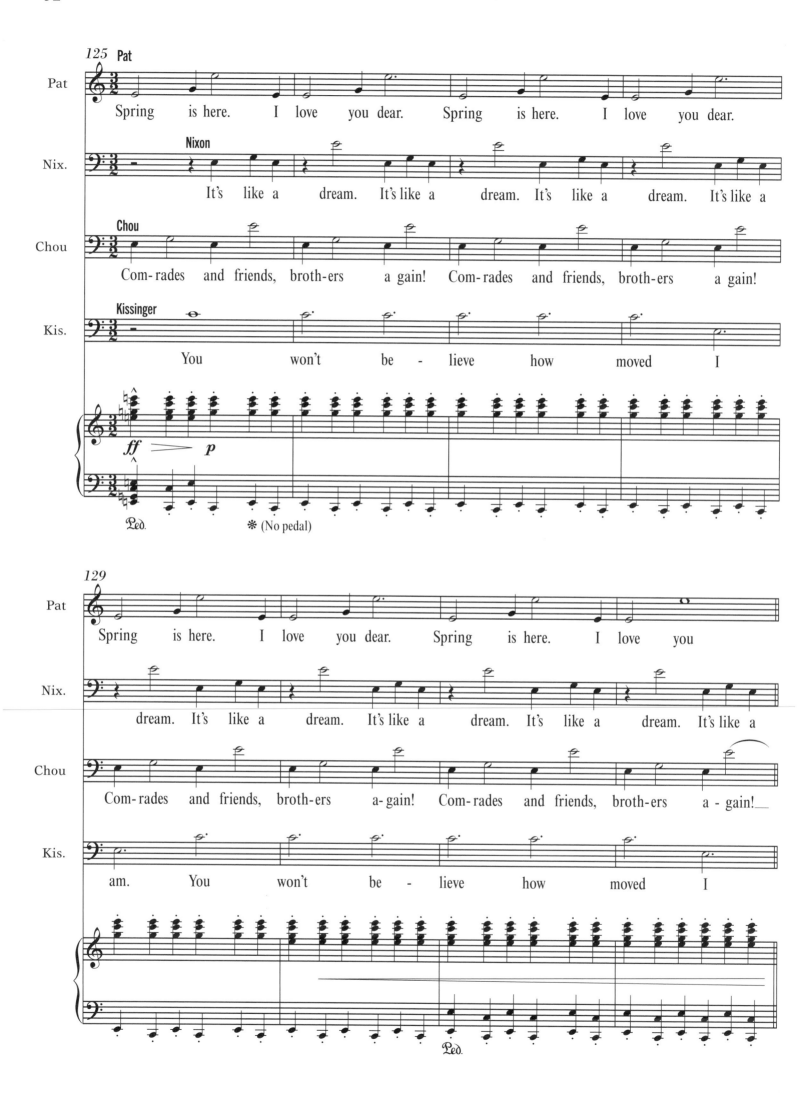

THE END OF JUNE, 1945
from DOCTOR ATOMIC

Libretto by
PETER SELLARS
drawn from original sources

Piano reduction by
CHITOSE OKASHIRO

Music by
JOHN ADAMS

A sus -tained neu- tron, neu- tron chain re- ac - tion

A sus -tained neu- tron, neu- tron chain re- ac - tion

A sus -tained neu- tron, neu- tron chain re- ac - tion

A sus -tained neu- tron, neu- tron chain re- ac - tion

A sus -tained neu- tron, neu- tron chain re- ac - tion

A sus -tained neu- tron, neu- tron chain re- ac - tion

UPPER VOICES

LOWER VOICES

mp

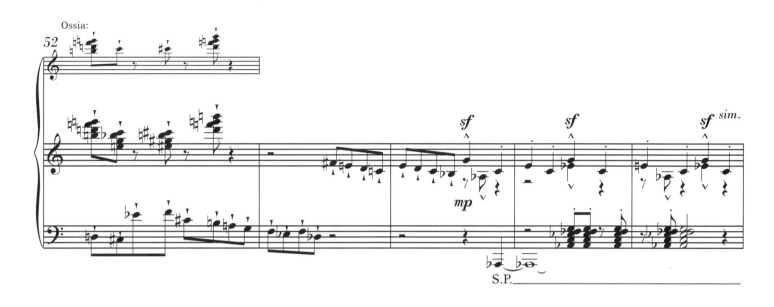

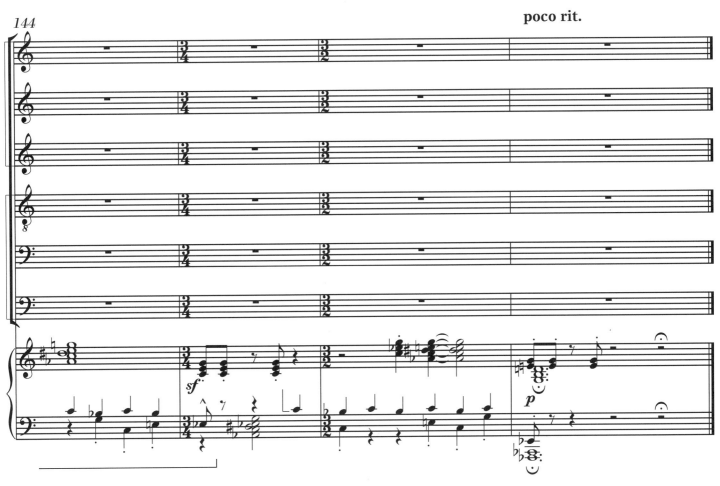

AT THE SIGHT OF THIS
from DOCTOR ATOMIC

Libretto by
PETER SELLARS
drawn from original sources

Piano reduction by
CHITOSE OKASHIRO

Music by
JOHN ADAMS

etc. Single note may be used instead of octave wherever octave leap in the piece is difficult. (R.H. in M.1-9 and L.H. in M.10-12)

* pronounced "dough"

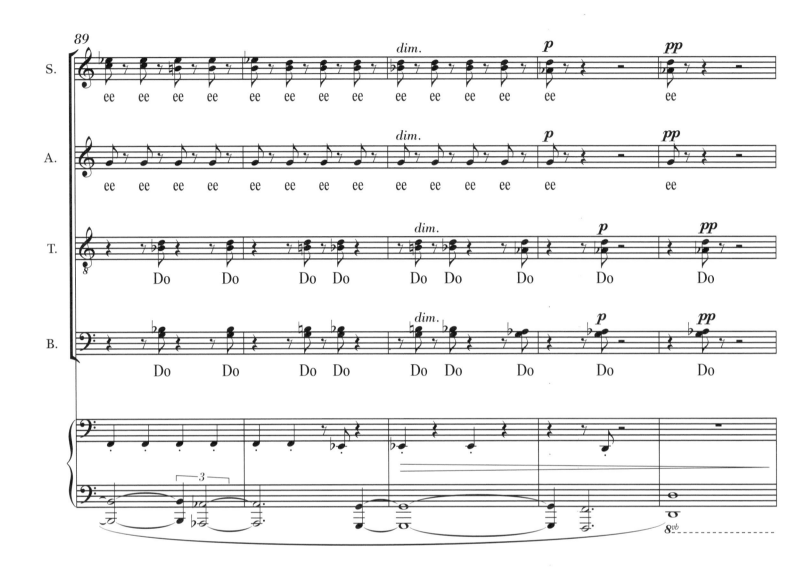

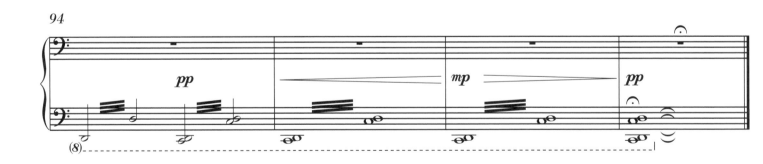

FLORES
from A FLOWERING TREE

Libretto adapted by
JOHN ADAMS *and* **PETER SELLARS**

Music by
JOHN ADAMS

Piano reduction by
CHITOSE OKASHIRO

* pronounced dō (as in "do re mi")

* can play on low D, or knock on wood